CAT
NIPS

BY RAY SHAW

AN
ESSANDESS
SPECIAL
EDITION
NEW YORK

CAT NIPS
SBN: 671-10526-4
Copyright, ©, 1970 by Ray Shaw.
All rights reserved.
Published by *Essandess Special Editions,*
a division of Simon & Schuster, Inc.,
630 Fifth Avenue, New York, N.Y. 10020,
and on the same day in Canada by
Simon & Schuster of Canada, Ltd.,
Richmond Hill, Ontario.
Printed in the U.S.A.

**You've been telling me for an hour
you'll be ready in a minute.**

**Officer, he left for a pack
of cigarettes three days ago
and I haven't seen him since.**

**Were you going
through my pants pockets again?**

You know,
you could use a shampoo.

It *is* becoming,
but I think
I'm a little too short
to carry it off.

I told you,
stop calling me
at the candy store.

**Why take a picture like this
just to let your mother know
we love her?**

Of course I'm a master plumber!
At these prices, I'd better be.

**If he deals me the king of hearts,
I'll have a royal flush.**

**Haven't you anything
that plays LPs?**

**Did they forget to serve the spoons
with the bouillon,
or is this a finger bowl?**

**I love you, Geranium,
now grow!!**

Where the devil is my secretary?

The recipe doesn't say how many loaves it'll make, but I think I can open a bakery.

**Don't be depressed honey.
Business will pick up
when the sun goes down.**

I said I'd *make* a will.
I didn't say I'd *sign* it.

**Did you ever see such carrying on
between two people their age?**

I never saw
so many degrees.
I don't think
I can afford
this doctor.

If I can only
lay my hands on a piano,
I've got it made.

The ad read, "comfortable for walking"
but I can't even sit in these.

I know it's wrong to eavesdrop,
but you learn so much this way.

I can't believe it's only a week
since I had a touch-up.

I never thought I'd make it
when I saw Miss South Dakota.

**Don't be angry, Killer.
I only did it to make you jealous.**

**I wonder if I could
find a man in Katmandu.**

**Your Honor,
do I look like the kind of girl
who would give false information?**

**Make your move, buddy,
before they take me to the old-age home.**

**If you want a Mayor
who doesn't dodge the issues,
vote for me.**

**Why do I *have*
to be Bar Mitzvahed?**

**Can't you think
of anything else?
I'm tired.**

You mean if we sign a confession, you'll let us go?

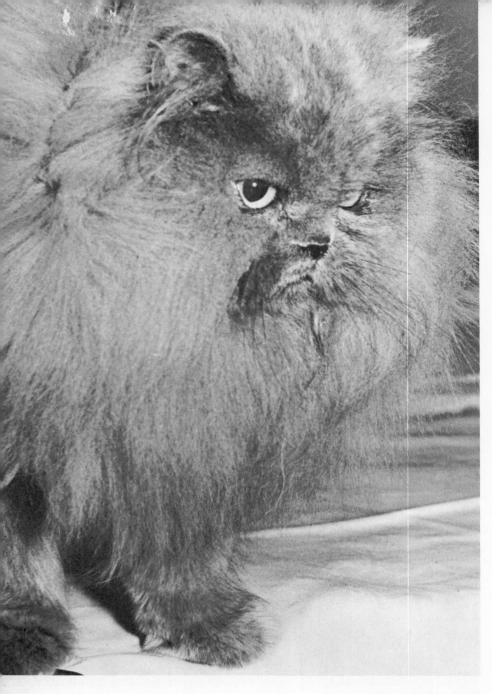

**You call yourself
a hairdresser?**

I'm using the blender for all my meals until I get my bridge fixed.

**I wish I'd never heard
of Fritz Kreisler.**

**There's that nosy Mrs. Manx
dishing the dirt with the postman.**

I've tried all the non-habit-forming
sleeping pills, Doctor,
but nothing seems to work.

Follow me, girls,
I think I hear male voices
in the next room.

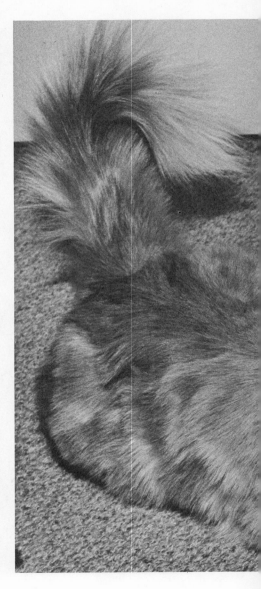

**Well would you do it
for two weeks on the Riviera?**

Tell them to send
anything with wheels.
I'm pooped!

**I said I'd like to do something different
to welcome springtime, but this is ridiculous.**

**And that's what I call
Ballin' the Jack.**

**Thirty days for calling
a policeman a no-no?**

I can never find
my charge-a-plate
when I need it.

It seems like I spend
half my life dusting knickknacks.

Remember, darling, the couple
that pets together, gets together.

**I wish they'd leave
so we could start our honeymoon.**

**To put a little fun
in your life, try dancing.**

**I must have left
the door key in my other suit.**

**One more A-Cat-amy award
and I'm going to retire.**

**How can we leave for Bermuda
if our Social Security checks don't come?**

**Do all fashion models
have to go
through this kind
of torture
to get started?**

**I don't think a few sips
could be called "falling off the wagon."**

Sure I'm rotten,
but I'm sensitive too.

**It's half isometric
and half yoga.**

I don't mind paying income tax,
but I resent having to become an accountant to do it.

**These stains
just won't come out,
even with the new
fast-acting detergents.**

**Not a drop of milk in the house,
and you come home loaded.**

Sign it "Two Lonely Hearts"
and see what kind of results it brings.

**This is the third day in a row
she's gotten out of
that big black limousine.**

**Alas, poor Yorick,
I knew him well.**

**Don't you love the way
I've furnished the place?**

**My only consolation is that
he's happier where he is now.**

**Knock off the sarcasm.
I had this coat *before*
those animals became scarce.**

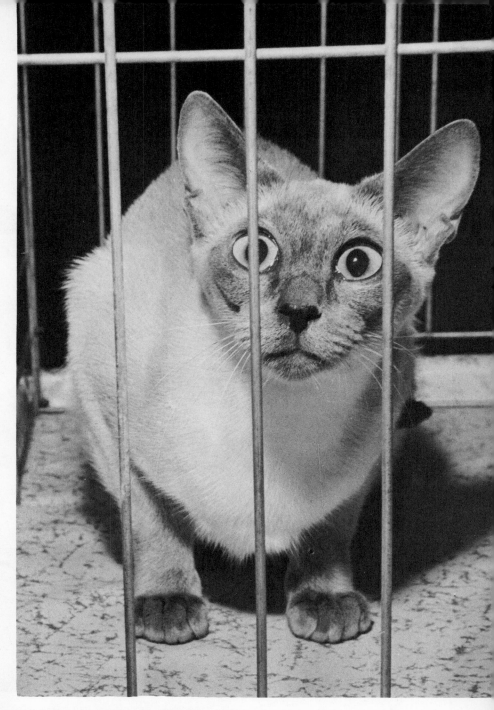

I'd rather you keep me here forever
than to make me go home with him!!

**I just can't flunk the finals.
Dad will cut off my allowance.**

When you said "some little bauble"
I wasn't expecting all this!

You can cross
in the traffic
if you want to,
but I think
you're sticking
your neck out.

**This is no ordinary hangover.
I think somebody
spiked my zombies.**

**Did someone say the office
will be closed tomorrow?**

**I'd like to use the powder room
and call my lawyer, in that order.**

I said, "Get out
and stay out!"

**Your rhumba just knocks me out,
Mr. Witherspoon.**

**And stop
at the cleaners
and bring home
my blue coat.**

**It never fails.
As soon as I come in here,
the phone rings.**

Let's make love, not war.

I've got to trade this one
in for an electric.

What makes you think
the meow-fia is out to get us?

You certainly do mix a great martini.